This journal belongs to

Introduction

Have you ever been told you are an old soul? Even people that aren't particularly into spirituality or the new age often use that term. It's a way of recognising the depth of compassion, presence and ancient wisdom that a certain soul type naturally carries. Lightworkers are a special type of old soul. They are people who love the light. Rather than living their lives focused on what they can get, they are naturally drawn to that which helps them give. Especially when that giving is about truth and inspiration, higher purpose and love.

Lightworkers are motivated by the things that help people to find ways out of darkness and suffering. Even if they don't think of themselves as healers, their loving and giving presence, and genuine goodwill towards all beings gives them a healing quality.

Even if they would rather not make waves (because they love peace), lightworkers tend to 'rock the boat'. This is part of their divine destiny. They are meant to bring in new belief systems and that can cause reactions from others who want to maintain the status quo. Not fitting in can be hard at first, but when a lightworker realises the freedom this brings, they often embrace their unique belief systems and feel delight in expressing themselves in many creative ways.

As they learn that they don't have to convince anyone of anything, and that they are free to express their truth and allow others to do with that what they will, lightworkers become a source of energy for many people, giving a sense of permission to believe in whatever one chooses. In a society largely conditioned by fear, this can be liberating, helping people change their lives for the better.

Lightworkers sometimes feel wearied by the weight of the world, as though the problems that they see all around them are somehow their responsibility to try and heal. They are genuinely motivated—as if spiritually programmed from the inside—to make a positive contribution to the planet. Instinctively, even if they don't use this sort of language, they recognise that part of their spiritual purpose is to raise the light quotient on earth. As they learn that they don't have to rescue anyone, but instead just shine their light through being themselves in positive ways, they can feel more optimistic.

An important lesson for lightworkers is to remember to take care of themselves first, to deal with their own issues. The more they are helping others, the more connection, peace and clarity they will need for themselves. When a lightworker starts to feel a sense of despair, doubt, fear or anxiety, it's a sign that they have become overloaded, quite possibly with energy that is not their own, and it is lowering their vibration. Like a bird trying to fly with rocks sitting on its wings, their natural lightness of spirit can start to feel heavy, as if they cannot attain 'lift off' or find their optimism, hope and laughter. When that happens, they need to switch off from others for a while, take a big step back into their inner world, perhaps through journaling, meditation and rest, and take some quality time to nurture themselves and attend to their own needs, so their lightness and energy can naturally return.

Lightworkers are regular human beings just like anyone else, and yet within them is something so unique that it sets them apart from the world in which they live. That inner difference is so profound that lightworkers may sometimes wonder if they are an alien in human clothing, looking like other people on the outside, but on the inside feeling somehow out of place in this world. For the special category of super-sensitive lightworkers that I refer to as star children, there is a sense of having come to this earth from another planet, galaxy or star altogether! Those souls often know they are here to serve and help others, yet can really struggle with the feeling that their own values of love, peace, higher consciousness and wisdom are so at odds with a human culture that often seems obsessed with gaining worldly power regardless of the spiritual cost. These special beings are helping to bring a refined consciousness to this planet, for the betterment of humanity, but they can often struggle to find their footing in the early part of their life, and even suffer from a feeling of spiritual displacement, wondering if they really belong here on Earth.

All lightworkers, including star children, are meant to be here on Earth but they often need encouragement to learn to embrace the earth as a loving soul guardian, feeling her generosity and protection before they can settle down with trust and really commit to their life journey. It often takes other lightworkers to recognise what a star child is going through and giving them the spiritual encouragement that they need. This can include a gentle but firm explanation that the negative feelings they are encountering are a result of their spiritual frequency adjusting to the emotional content created by the wounds of humanity. They will be able to handle their feelings more skilfully in time. They will learn how to spiritually 'surf' the collective emotional field of humanity, rather than drown in it, but it can take a little while to master that skill. Meditation often helps to speed up that process, as does any kind of therapeutic support in learning how to process emotions in a healthy way.

All lightworkers, particularly star children, can struggle with depression or addiction, or a feeling of homesickness and, during deep crisis, perhaps even suicidal feelings. Getting as much support as they can during these times is so important. Along with meditation that they enjoy (and there are many different types of meditation to explore), therapy with a professionally trained and open-minded psychotherapist can be of great help whilst they learn to ground their spirit in the world. I have found that Jungian analysts can be wonderful supporters for people on the spiritual path, but choosing a therapist is a heart-felt, intuitive choice that needs to resonate for each individual.

This is important, because apart from the fact that lightworkers are beautiful beings and do not deserve to suffer, they also have a unique purpose to fulfil on this planet – helping to bring the higher frequencies from their spiritual home and manifesting them on the earth. We really need them on earth!

A helpful way for all lightworkers to ground and more easily manifest their divine life mission is to fall in love with nature. Trusting in nature as a 'soul mother' brings comfort, guidance and the reassurance they are safe, needed and really do belong here at a deep, spiritual level. Meditation, journaling, sacred rituals and conscious dance are other ways lightworkers can be reminded that they still have their spiritual home right inside of them (which they always do), even whilst they are learning to manifest that inner consciousness in their outer lives. The Universe is kind to these beings and when they ask for help, the right information, teacher or support system will pop up for them. It is just a matter of trusting in the journey.

If you resonate with the path of the lightworker, know that you are not crazy just because you see things differently – even if you see things differently to absolutely every person around you! It's okay. You are as you are meant to be, and you were designed with a higher loving divine purpose in mind. Your task is to be wholly, truthfully and joyfully yourself, and to take your journey, loving what you love and asking the Universe each day to connect you more deeply to the divine energy of love, truth, wisdom and presence that lives within you.

The Universe knows your inner path and purpose—even when you might be feeling confused about what to do or where to go—and it is always guiding you so that you can do the work you came here to do, in your own unique way. The Universe can and will lead you each step of the way to fulfil the inner destiny that you sense but cannot always clearly see or articulate. Trusting in the intuitions of your heart will help you find patience and peace as you take the journey step by step. You may even notice in time that your own soul growth is inspiring and nourishing to those around you. Without realising it, they are taking refuge in your growing light. When you relax and trust in yourself and in the Universe, there is so much spiritual healing that just pours through you for the greater good.

With love and blessings,

Alana

The universal law of resonance and vibration explains why, as lightworkers, we deal with the negative in our world, and in us, as best we can, but when we have the choice, will surround ourselves with truth, beauty and healing energies. We may do this by spending time in nature and clean, uplifting environments or meditating regularly and connecting with a source of inner peace. We raise our vibration and we feel better for it.

When working with light, you need to listen to your body. Rest and pace yourself. Learn how to expand, but also how to recover and integrate. Take your time to replenish so that when you give, it feels like you are also receiving, rather than depleting yourself. If giving feels tiring, you need to receive more. Balance will help you experience joy in sharing your light with the world.

As a lightworker, you won't always be understood, as it is not a mainstream vocation at this phase in human spiritual evolution. Those that do understand you will be all the more precious to you, and you will be benefiting humanity as a whole, and that is a precious gift for which the Universe will reward you in its own brilliant and perfect way.

The Universe will provide you with every support when you are walking your path. Opportunities will come to you. If they do not, then you need to ask yourself this question: 'Am I allowing myself to follow a heart-centred path. And if so, is this just a question of trusting in universal timing?'

Your path will always find you. You may feel as if you are bumbling about in the dark, with not a clue as to what you are here to do, but here is a truth – you are already on your path. Whether it makes sense to you, seems practical, or makes sense to another, doesn't matter. When you are on the right path for you, life conspires to help you in ways that for another person would not be possible.

You are part of a new consciousness presently emerging on earth. This is the consciousness of inclusion, of love. You are a co-creator of this new era of love, healing and consciousness on our planet. You matter. Your presence, your thoughts, your feelings make a difference to us all.

Love is all things. It is boldness and action, gentleness and peace. Remember this as you build your 'lighthouse'. This is the space inside where your inner radiance can burn with divine passion, piercing through darkness, offering hope and direction to many who are lost. This is your soul. This is your heart.

It is time to accept the loving gauntlet being thrown down by the Universe and take your hands off the controls of your life! Detach and be curious. The Universe will show you exactly what you need and remove what you do not. The Universe loves you and wants only the best and most beautiful life experience for you. Trust it enough to let that happen now.

A prayer of trust and surrender for your path: Through unconditional love and divine mercy, I surrender my life into the loving hands of the Universe to align me with higher will and the most beautiful expression of my life journey.

Our 'positive karma' is seen in the skills and talents we have mastered over many lifetimes. Also, when opportunities flow easily, and healing happens swiftly, there is a sense of positive karma, an easy grace that effortlessly takes place in your life. This is what happens when we are clear enough of our past pain to have little resistance between us and the natural flow of life.

Healing Exercise: What do I need to release now?

Healing with the First Ray of Power

SPIRITUAL GUIDANCE

The first of the three major universal energy rays is the First Ray of Power. The Universe emanates the First Ray of Power to help us. It is the energy of conscious destruction. It can be used in a healthy way to eliminate what needs to be released – often something from the past or an old habit of thought or behaviour that isn't supporting our soul growth – and to allow for a fresh start, freed from previous limitations.

The First Ray also carries the frequency of leadership. It can help you to stand in the truth of your light, so others can find their way by it. It helps to strengthen your willpower, so you can accomplish any task you choose. The ascended master associated with the First Ray is El Morya who now brings you his blessing and encourages you to believe in your own strength and take the initiative on what matters most to you.

When the First Ray of Power draws your attention, you are being asked to take stock and release whatever psychological, emotional or physical material is holding you back from taking the next step on your journey. The Universe knows that you are ready. Sometimes you just need to summon faith in yourself and let change happen.

HEALING PROCESS

Write a list of at least three things you are willing to release, even if you feel you need spiritual assistance from the Universe to do so. They might be attitudes, negative belief systems, a recurring inner criticism towards yourself or someone else or a situation in your life, those things could also be an addictive behaviour, a fear of loss, rejection or failure, or even a willingness to clear your home or give away some items that you don't use anymore and that others may love.

When you are ready, say this prayer: *I ask for divine assistance in releasing these things from my life* (read your list). *I ask for this help with mercy, compassion and grace. May I let go in order to allow greater blessings into my life, for the greatest good of all sentient beings. So be it.*

Take a few moments to rest your hand on your heart and feel what it is like to soften and relax, with trust that the Universe is going to show you how to let go gracefully and without fear, so that you can move into the next step of your soul journey. You may like to imagine what it feels like to no longer see these things as 'issues' in your life, as though the solution is already unfolding. Remember the more courageous you are, the more the Universe can step in and assist you.

When you are ready, finish your healing process by saying the invocation below.

INVOCATION

I now accept, of my own free will, the blessing and grace of the First Ray of Power in my life. Through unconditional love and divine mercy, I surrender my life into the loving hands of the Universe to align me with higher will and the most beautiful expression of my life journey. I call upon the loving assistance of the genuine ascended master El Morya in all aspects of this process and ask that the First Ray of Power be expressed in ways that serve the greatest good on this planet, that all beings may walk their true divine path. Through divine grace, so be it.

When you are working through big challenges, it is often a sign that you are on an advanced spiritual path. Must you always have struggle in your life as an advanced soul? Of course not! As you master your lessons, you will find you develop an ability to live your life more peacefully. However, it would be incorrect to interpret a struggle as a sign that you are not progressing spiritually.

We clear karma by learning to trust and relax, by choosing not to punish ourselves with shame, guilt, fear or unworthiness, by continuing to balance our efforts with a surrender into divine grace.

The mainstream is still operating in a fear-based energy. With increased sensitivity, you can at times be more affected by this. You can overcome this without shutting down. Respond with a loving discipline. You might meditate, journal, dance, create art, listen to music, exercise, have a bath, or spend time in nature to bring yourself back to balance.

There is a belief system based on fear, doubt and distrust that is known as 'mass consciousness.' It says that if you dare to stand up and live your truth, you'll be lost and alone, humiliated, rejected or even destroyed. You are being guided to unplug from that system of beliefs. You are capable of a more creative, loving and soul-satisfying way of living.

No matter how others may resist or criticise your choices (perhaps your new ideas take you away from the world they feel comfortable in), your higher guidance encourages you to keep opening your mind to a more loving higher reality.

Trust yourself. You are thinking in ways that do not belong to mass consciousness. It can seem scary at first, but once you realise the benefits gained from unplugging, you will enjoy the process much more. Opportunities and connections can then open to you in ways that defy your old beliefs.

You were born to bring a new vibration of awareness to this planet. You will find those who can benefit and even love you for this difference, and those who are challenged or fearful of you for it. Either way, you can love and approve of yourself, nourish relationships that support you and have compassionate detachment from those that do not, without compromising who you are in truth.

An affirmation for protection: Of my own free will, I now ask for spiritual intervention and divine protection through the guidance that loves me unconditionally.

You are in a process of becoming more of heaven on earth. Sometimes, there are growing pains alongside the joy such growth brings. The Universe is very much with you, encouraging you, believing in you.

A healing prayer to the Divine Feminine: I ask for the blessings of nurture, development, evolution and growth for the best and most beautiful divine destiny. I am guided, protected and assisted to become all that I can be. With gratitude and trust in the flow of my life, I relax and take the journey. As I do so, I help to bring calm and consciousness to the world for the greater good. So be it.

It's time to end the frustration of repeating old patterns. You are ready to break through into a new way of life! Feel inspired, be energised and focus on your dreams and desires. Take steps to manifest them on the physical plane. Believe your success is inevitable.

Divine masculine energy exists within all men and women. It rallies the spirit and responds in times when you may feel drained, taken advantage of, or overwhelmed by too many choices and demands. It cuts through the confusion that comes with choice and priority setting. It refuses to be distracted and keeps you from being dissuaded from your life purpose.

Let the Divine Masculine become strong in you – he can be your guide, protector and defender. Trust when he says no to something or someone. Trust when he says, 'You are ready for this!' and encourages you to act. As you trust in him, you will trust yourself to be visible. You will shine your light without fear.

A dark mystery is one that helps us learn that even if things don't seem to be working out according to the timing or the methods that we believe necessary, the light and love of Spirit are unfailing. If a door is closed in your face, it is the wrong door for you! Divine love will ensure that the right door opens at the right time.

Healing Exercise: What am I attracting into my life?

Healing with the Second Ray of Love-Wisdom

SPIRITUAL GUIDANCE

The second of the three major universal energy rays is the Ray of Love-Wisdom. The Ray of Love-Wisdom is the energy of the open and loving heart of the Universe. It is an emanation of the Buddha's loving mind of compassion and the open heart of the Christ. This second ray is inclusive, drawing all things towards it with an invisible magnetism. It is gifted to you at this time to help you attract the people, opportunities and teachings that will help you succeed in your life mission.

This ray will help you focus your consciousness in your heart. It will bring to consciousness any unresolved matters of the heart for healing. This includes not only issues of relationship, but also any issues around trusting your heart to lead you. This ray will help heal your heart in an affirming and nurturing way. It will also help you learn to trust your heart as a source of wisdom. It is easier to feel our wisdom, which is always non-judgmental, when the heart is freed from bitterness, grief, sorrow, fear or other pain from unresolved past experiences. When the heart feels peaceful and clear, it is easier to recognise our wisdom, the voice of inner guidance. It is also easier to trust in the generosity of the Universe if our heart is not shrouded in negative filters based on fearful societal conditioning.

The Second Ray of Love-Wisdom is known specifically as the ray of teachers and educators. You are encouraged to trust that you have a message to share that is helpful and possibly even educational for others. Honour the energy of the teacher in your life with humility and grace. What you have to share has value and can be so helpful for those who are ready to receive your message. Let the Universe choose your audience. All you need to do is share your message without attachment as to who receives it, or when. This is part of your soul purpose as a teacher and guide from a place of love-wisdom.

HEALING PROCESS

Write a list of at least three things you would like to increase or attract into your life. These could be material things, but they could also be an attitude—such as an attitude of abundance, gratitude and grace, and trust in the generosity of the Universe—that will naturally attract *many* wonderful things to your life, even whilst you are enjoying the beauty of being free to focus on the content of your heart emanation.

When you have completed your list, read each item aloud. After reading your list say:

By the love of Christ (touch your heart for a moment) *and the wisdom of Buddha* (touch your forehead for a moment), *I open myself to receive with dignity and for the greatest good. I accept all goodness, blessing and abundance into my life, with joy. May I share my good fortune with generosity and grace. May all beings be happy and free.*

Imagine, feel, sense or pretend that the generosity of the Universe is pouring down through you, like a golden river of love, light and beauty. Allow this golden river to fill you and then flow into the earth, touching the hearts and minds of all in need.

When you are ready, finish by saying the invocation below.

INVOCATION

I now accept, of my own free will, the blessing and grace of the Second Ray of Love-Wisdom in my life. Through unconditional love and divine mercy, I open my heart with joy to the magnetic and creative field of attraction. I gratefully open to abundance in all ways with trust, wisdom and serenity. The Universe provides all that I want and need with grace, love and perfect timing. Thank you, Universe! I call on the loving assistance of the genuine ascended masters known as the Buddha and the Christ in all aspects of this process so that all beings can receive the loving benefit of this spiritual gift, according to divine compassion. Through divine grace, so be it.

*When you encounter darkness, how you respond can make either the dark
or the light victorious. You can choose doubt and fear – or you can force the
darkness to serve the light, by choosing trust and faith. You are spiritually
advanced enough to trust unconditionally.*

You are willing to continue your path, even when you are not seeing immediate results, because in your heart you know it is right. You know that, even when the Universe guides you into challenging territory, you shall benefit, grow in divine power, and become the amazing being you are destined to be.

As we realise how we have grown through experience, turning what was once a source of pain into spiritual light, we masterfully transform our deepest pain into our greatest growth and spiritual accomplishment. We become true spiritual alchemists, releasing light from darkness.

As you learn to put more faith in love than in fear, your trust becomes increasingly unconditional, and you find the light even through the dark. You can help heal yourself and others from victim consciousness, showing that inner peace is possible, even with the unpredictable twists and turns of life.

Creation doesn't happen in the past or in the future. It happens in the here and now through the choices you make in each moment. Even now, in reading this message, you are choosing to be present, to bring your energy into the eternal now, stimulating the law of attraction into action.

An affirmation for now: I choose to dwell in the peace of this moment,
where all is unfolding according to a secret divine perfection.

A prayer for remembrance and relaxation: I am loved and provided for, and all is happening for my greatest fulfilment.

In preparation for radical growth, there can be temporary disorder and chaos. Whilst the mind may worry something is going wrong, the spirit knows this is a way for the old to disassemble so the new can be formed.

There is no need to attempt to impose your own sense of order upon the greater plan. You do not need to seek solutions, for there is no problem here in need of solving. What has been is being cleared away in preparation for the next chapter in your life. Have faith. All is well.

To feel inner peace during times of transition or chaos, you must trust in your own inner knowing of what appears to be.

The Universe knows what you need and is in the process of delivering it to you now.
All is happening for a greater purpose. You can flow with change in loving trust.

If, like a newborn colt learning to stand steady on shaky legs, you are not sure of your strength, be reassured. The new self you are experiencing will grow strong and powerful in due course. Let confidence in your new self emerge. Reflect upon how different you are now to a year or even a month ago. Be curious about who you are now.

A prayer of good will and protection for all: May all the people and ideas that are in need of protection so they may grow into their divine fullness be blessed and supported by unconditional love. Through divine grace, so be it.

Your dreams want you just as much as you want them. Grounding helps you bring your dreams to life in your world, for the benefit of many.

Grounding is a chance to check in with what is happening in your physical life and make sure you are giving appropriate time and energy to what really matters to your heart.

Practise soothing and calming yourself so that you can return yourself to a contented, trusting and peaceful state of being. This can be done by talking to yourself in a gentle, loving, encouraging voice, reassuring yourself that everything is working out according to a higher plan and that you are very loved.

Healing Exercise: What practical manifestation does my soul want to create now?

Third Ray of Creative Intelligence

SPIRITUAL GUIDANCE

The last of the three main energy rays of the Universe is the Third Ray of Creative Intelligence.

This ray will help you gain practicality to organise and manifest an idea or vision in the world. It gives you the drive and the means to implement your plans. When this ray is active in our lives, we want to act, to bring something to life – not just to know or feel, but to do.

When the Third Ray gets our attention, it means there is a vision or dream that wants to come to life in the world, and you are being encouraged to take the steps necessary for this to happen. You will need to trust in your capability and competence, your confidence and practical, down-to-earth common sense, even if these are not always your strongest qualities. If you doubt your ability to achieve all that you dream of, remember that sometimes the Universe puts dreams in our hearts to help us develop strengths that are dormant within us. You will grow into whatever is needed to bring your dream to life if you are willing to let the Universe help you!

The challenge with this ray is to take things one step at a time. Allow the Universe to help you find the patience, persistence and sense of humour that will help you stick to the process of creation. Do not try to do too much at once, nor give up before you even start! Don't allow your project to get too complicated, instead break it down into steps so that you don't feel overwhelmed. The Universe wants to help you ground and manifest more of your light. Trust that the Universe knows what it is doing, and that you are part of this creative flow.

This ray also relates to business and finance. It can help heal the tension that many feel between spirituality and financial abundance. It helps us recognise that the spirit feels joy in successful physical-world endeavours, particularly those that serve love. When a situation is a win-win for all involved, there is no reason at all to hold back from material success. It can be celebrated and enjoyed, whilst you maintain your focus on the true motivation for the work – which is love.

HEALING PROCESS

Take a moment to reflect on where you would like your physical-world experience to better 'match' the beauty of your inner-world visions. Are there practical steps for your health, work, love life or creative soul path that you feel you could be taking? Do you want to bring something to life but aren't sure what the next step should be, or when to take the next steps? Write these questions or intentions down.

When you are ready, say the following prayer: *I open to divine grace, and the assistance of the angels and the Earth Mother, to fully manifest my inner purpose in the outer world. Please assist me with grace, mercy and abundance to create my heart's desire, especially in the following matters now. I trust I will recognise which steps to take, and the timing in which to take them, through divine support and help. So be it.*

Read your list aloud. Then read the invocation below to complete the healing process.

INVOCATION

I now accept, of my own free will, the blessing and grace of the Third Ray of Creative Intelligence. I thank the Universe for all assistance in turning my spiritual aspirations into successful, practical, real-world manifestations of light, grace, love and empowerment. I gratefully receive the unconditionally loving intervention of Archangel Chamuel to recover and express all talents and abilities meant to help me fulfil my mission. Thank you, Universe, for helping me to manifest my divine dreams. I ask that, in unconditional love, this ray be made available to all who can benefit from it, according to divine wisdom, mercy and compassion for the greatest good. So be it.

A prayer for grounding: I enjoy being present, with my body and my breath, receiving spiritual light and shining it through my heart into the world. I love my body and my senses, my soul and my heart. They are all avenues for my spirit to experience and express in this world for the greatest good. May all living beings feel helpful grounding through unconditional love.

Some people are hesitant to let go of what they know – even if it is emotional suffering and mental anguish. Fear prevents them from being willing to trust in the loving hand reaching out to them. You can make a different and more trusting choice.

A prayer for the dark night of the soul: Bring me the peace and spiritual blessing that I need to be freed from darkness and opened to the sweet light of love's truth. May all beings caught in darkness be assisted by unconditional love, to see, feel and know that the path of love is theirs forever.

It is time to gently undo the patterns of attempting to fit in. Instead, trust that you are exactly as you were meant to be. Leave past hurts and rejection behind. You no longer need them to grow.

Rest. Open up and allow. Be patient and trust in your process. If emotional content arises, and you are concerned you might be falling back into old habits, do not be afraid. Find ways to creatively express what you are feeling. Explore your personal expression to allow for spiritual expansion.

Ascension can be a wild ride! Anything is possible. The past is not an indicator. The future is not set. This is the moment to cultivate your deepest feelings of spiritual love and peace.

An Ascension Prayer: I call upon the unconditionally loving guidance
that can assist me through my ascension process with mercy, grace,
protection and support. I accept this opportunity to grow spiritually and
shift from one reality to a higher vibrational reality. May I be held in
tenderness and compassion as I release lower vibrational patterning and
embody my authentic divinity. Through my own free will, so be it.

No matter how mixed up and consumed by darkness the world may seem at times,
there are so many powers of light working to see the earth and humanity through this
most interesting time and into the new age of spiritual enlightenment.

If you are uncertain about what is happening in your life now, don't fret. Sometimes a smaller desire must be sacrificed for the attainment of the greater vision. Be at peace. Know that all beings shine at the right time, and so shall you.

Self-doubt can be a habit that is hard to break. Ultimately, it won't stop you, but it's easier to fulfil your purpose when you acknowledge your own goodness and talent. Realise that you are enough and that you have something of value to offer. It is time to let go of your fear of failure and any concern about your ability and your right to live a happy and fulfilled life of success. The Universe believes in you.

A love letter to the Universe: Universe, I love you. How can I serve you?
I accept love's protection and love's purpose in my heart, in my life.
Love empowers and protects me, gives me purpose and passion, peace
and play. You give me so much, let me give back, from my heart, to you.

An affirmation of forgiveness to free the soul: I forgive myself and all others for our human mistakes. I choose to honour a mistake as a chance to learn and an opportunity from the Divine to grow more loving.

You must believe in yourself. You don't have to force a door to open. In perfect time, according to divine grace, all doors will open for you.

Free yourself with love, not fear. You may need to lock doors to the past behind you.
With divine empowerment, you can completely and utterly allow the past to be over.
You will find that new doors can then be unlocked for you.

You are elevating your vibration towards the frequency of limitless supply and unconditional love. Spiritually, you are reaching for a high level of attainment. Past pain and self-defeating behaviours shall no longer have a place in your heart.

Duguay

Healing Exercise: Paradigm Shift

When your old belief systems cannot keep up with what your soul wants to create, they need to evolve!

SPIRITUAL GUIDANCE

Sometimes who you once were, and what you once thought, is just not 'high frequency' enough to support who you are becoming and where you are meant to go. In such transitions, the mind is not able to fathom the new reality, so it can feel like a frightening and exhilarating leap of faith (or absolute craziness!) to put your trust in something that you cannot yet see, know or recognise, yet in your heart, really want to experience. This is where the soul begins to pull in higher frequencies of consciousness—more loving, less fearful, more open, less controlling, more willing, less resistant. Those new frequencies will conflict with the old ones. Once your mind warned you to stay safe and keep your head down. Now, suddenly, your heart is urging you to take a leap of faith and open yourself up to the Universe! Well, of course, you may be confused and wondering which voice to trust.

You are undergoing radical growth in your belief systems. Now is the time to challenge old attitudes and question previous expectations. You are in an extraordinary time. Great leaps forward can be made in a moment. The world you thought you knew can suddenly break open and a new world can become your reality. It's okay to go with the loving and fearless voices that are breaking free within you. In time, that will become your new reality. However, you will be going through the transition between old fear and new trust for a little while. That is alright. Just recognise what is happening. An inner mental alchemy of new consciousness is making itself felt within you–allow yourself to be patient, steady and attentive. Act on the voices of love, and be kind, but firm, with the voices of fear.

The Universe knows your belief systems need an upgrade, so you can be ready for what is coming to you–your own divine destiny. Trust in the timing and the process and don't be afraid to embrace the unknown, as your own beautiful soul manifests its inner wisdom.

Any time you feel stressed or confused about which inner voice to listen to–fear or love–remember that love is wisdom and fear is unresolved past pain. Then repeat the invocation below and give yourself permission to relax with trust in yourself and the Universe.

INVOCATION

Through divine grace and unconditional love, I open my mind to the higher truth of love. May my mind be cleansed from conditioning and gently opened to the light of love. I am willing to unlearn what no longer serves me. I am willing to receive teachings and information, guidance and assistance from those beings of pure light and unconditional love that can now assist me on my life journey. May my paradigm shift bring me closer to peace, love, empowerment and happiness. May this process be held in guardianship by the Universe, with grace, mercy and tenderness. Through my own free will, so be it.

You may feel you need to sacrifice yourself for others, but you are just as much in need of love as any other being on this planet. When you are full and overflowing, what you share with others can enhance you and them. It is not a choice between what nurtures you and what nurtures others, as if those were competing needs. In the realm of Christ Consciousness, what nurtures you is nurturing for all.

It can be a challenge to learn to love another in a way that does not harm you. Perhaps you learned that love was about making yourself less to help another feel like more. This is not love. Nor is it consciously chosen sacrifice. That is a heart acting out its scars from the past. Your heart deserves to experience real love.

You have as much right to experience love, respect and forgiveness as another. Sharing love in any way brings you closer to your spiritual mission this lifetime. It also attracts prosperity and abundance. Let the love in. You do not have to suffer to grow now, you just need to let love flow.

*Part of your divine purpose is to develop the power of your mind and use it
for healing.*

Whatever your struggles may be, they will soon reveal themselves to be nothing more than steps along your path to the sweetest blossoming of your soul. Be patient. Rest with a rose light in your heart, for healing energy is flowing into you, now.

The Law of Efficiency encourages us to work smarter, rather than always working harder. It is like learning to allow a wave to carry you to shore, rather than swimming the entire way with your own efforts alone – or even against the current, which would make the journey even harder. Give yourself permission to tune in and flow with the universal energies of life.

To hitch your wagon to the Universe, you need to listen. This means tuning in to what feels right or wrong at any given time. Sometimes, you will want to push forward, yet your intuitive knowing will guide you to rest. Sometimes, you will want to hide from a challenge – and yet know in your bones it is time to step up and shine with boldness, despite the fear you may feel.

The Universe has natural flow, cycles and timing that assure us it supports every dream we dare to dream – and that each can come to fruition in due course. It may not look exactly as you expect, but if you have set it in motion with desire and intention, it is karmic law that it finds expression.

It takes spiritual maturity to cede to wisdom greater than your own immediate understanding. It is so wise to work with life and its cycles, rather than believing you must struggle and strain to be heard, loved, rewarded and inspired. You have that maturity within you. Trust now. Trust that all will come in time.

A prayer for spiritually intelligent surrender: Please bless and guide me now in all ways for maximum success, joy, and divinely inspired fulfilment. May my efforts be wise and surrendered, powerful and efficient. May all beings be assisted through divine mercy to discover the path of grace and divine efficiency.

What do you love enough to overcome any obstacle to attain it? What motivates and inspires you? Not what seems possible or practical, but what is authentic? A bird yearns to fly because that is its divine nature and purpose. You too have divine nature and purpose, and your heart holds the clue. What feels most like you?

If you have a dream in your heart, know it has been placed there for divine purpose. What you dream and desire contains the seed of divinity. It is meant to help attract your life mission and fulfil it with love, joy, creativity and pleasure.

Many souls who are different and unique were not understood, acknowledged or valued for who they were as children. Instead, they were encouraged to conform, to change, to be other than their true self in order to be loved. You are being encouraged, instead, to distil your essence, to become even more of you. Accept the love that created you as you.

Sometimes, whilst a treasure is emerging from the depths of your being, it will be coated in the pain of the past. You may need to dig a little, to crack open the coating of a wound and free the treasure that temporarily became trapped in that pain. When you release the pain, you free the treasure once locked within it.

A prayer for global healing: May the Golden Light heal all beings of fear and doubt, gently bestowing mercy, compassion and the loving reassurance of divine presence into the hearts of all. Through divine grace and my own free will, so be it.

The Universe is lovingly listening to every thought and feeling in your heart and mind. When you intentionally speak to the Universe and ask your higher guidance to help you with an issue, this is a powerful way to call the light into your life. It works.

It is spiritually mature to trust the greater guiding power of the Universe to direct
your course, yet destiny is not something that just happens to you. It is something
you co-create as a living, spiritual being with free will and divine love beating in your
heart. Use your voice. Affirm your blessings and your beautiful visions.

Don't be afraid to speak your dreams, desires, wishes and fantasies.
Sometimes it is only in daring to speak them aloud that we really
understand what we want. This can be a terrifying, liberating, exciting and
life-changing moment! It is the moment that we grow into a spiritual adult,
becoming willing to take responsibility for our own life journey.

It is time for you to have the experience of seeing your intention blossom into manifestation. This does not mean you have to make things happen. The Universe unfolds according to its own genius. But you are responsible for your words, beliefs and intentions – they are the seeds of your personal creations. The Universe then responds in its own wise and powerful way.

Will you speak your heart truths now? Feel your words moving the energy from deep within, transforming your truth into sound and releasing it as intent into the Universe! Don't worry about finding the perfect words – just speak freely from your heart. Give yourself permission to express your deepest desires and then let go and trust.

The right answers will come. Be willing to change your viewpoint to perceive the truth of the matter. If a system is working for you, that's great. If it needs to be changed, don't be afraid to go into the chaos of creativity and try different ways until you discover what will work better for you now.

Love is an empowering, motivating force far stronger than fear.

Channel your emotional and mental energies into worthy projects and
practise balancing your intensity with lightness of heart and playfulness so
you don't become harsh or despairing if things appear not to be working
out. Then, your faith can remind you that love always finds a way.

A prayer for all sentient beings: May all sentient beings feel safe and consciously held in a loving divine order, according to the great plan of love. Through my own free will, so be it.